World Trade

Edited by Aaron Carr

www.av2books.com

MEDIA ENHANCED BOOKS
AV²
BY WEIGL™
ADDED VALUE • AUDIO VISUAL

AV² provides enriched content that supplements and complements this book. Weigl's AV² books strive to create inspired learning and engage young minds in a total learning experience.

Your AV² Media Enhanced books come alive with...

Audio
Listen to sections of the book read aloud.

Key Words
Study vocabulary, and complete a matching word activity.

Video
Watch informative video clips.

Quizzes
Test your knowledge.

Embedded Weblinks
Gain additional information for research.

Slide Show
View images and captions, and prepare a presentation.

Try This!
Complete activities and hands-on experiments.

... and much, much more!

Go to **www.av2books.com**, and enter this book's unique code.

BOOK CODE

B460124

AV² by Weigl brings you media enhanced books that support active learning.

Download the AV² catalog at
www.av2books.com/catalog

AV² Online Navigation on page 48

Published by AV² by Weigl
350 5th Avenue, 59th Floor
New York, NY 10118

Websites: www.av2books.com   www.weigl.com

Library of Congress Control Number: 2014940095

ISBN 978-1-4896-1102-4 (hardcover)
ISBN 978-1-4896-1103-1 (softcover)
ISBN 978-1-4896-1104-8 (single-user eBook)
ISBN 978-1-4896-1105-5 (multi-user eBook)

Printed in the United States of America in North Mankato, Minnesota
1 2 3 4 5 6 7 8 9 0 18 17 16 15 14

052014
WEP090514

Weigl acknowledges Getty Images as its primary image supplier for this title.

Every reasonable effort has been made to trace ownership and to obtain permission to reprint copyright material. The publishers would be pleased to have any errors or omissions brought to their attention so that they may be corrected in subsequent printings.

Project Coordinator: Aaron Carr
Art Director: Terry Paulhus

World Trade

CONTENTS

Introduction to World Trade

Trade is the buying and selling of products and services. Domestic trade is the trading done within a nation. International, or world, trade is trading that occurs among nations. The process of trading is key to civilization, whether it is a purchase at a corner store or a trade agreement made by heads of state. When people buy and sell goods in marketplaces, they also build relationships.

Importance of Trade

"The world economy is the outcome of countless trade decisions by businesses and governments."

Development of Trade

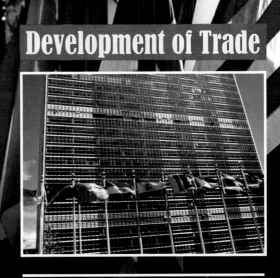

"Ever since World War II ended, trade has grown quickly, but not all nations have enjoyed the benefits equally."

Trade in Action

"Many trade groups involve countries in specific regions, such as Europe or North America."

Issues of Trade

"Increasingly, people are demanding that trade should not hurt the environment and should

Importance of Trade

KEY CONCEPTS

1 Consumers and Producers

2 Supply and Demand

3 Capital

4 Free and Protected Trade

5 Developed and Developing Countries

Trade is based on the needs and decisions of individuals and groups. Individuals make trading decisions such as which car to buy. Officials at international companies make other kinds of choices, such as selecting a security team to protect their Internet data. Cars are products, or goods, which are owned and consumed. Security is a service that is experienced.

1 Consumers and Producers

The world economy is the outcome of countless trade decisions. These decisions are made by businesses and governments. Yet, even the world economy operates on some basic principles that reflect the behavior of individuals.

When choosing goods and services, people act as consumers. Those who make the goods and provide the services are producers. A barber is a producer when he or she offers the service of cutting hair. The barber acts as a consumer when selecting a sandwich for lunch at a restaurant. Restaurants offer both goods and services. They also consume goods, such as the lettuce and tomatoes used for sandwich toppings.

The barber selects lunch based on what is important at the moment. That could involve the barber's craving for certain tastes, the healthfulness of the sandwiches on the menu, or the cost. In general, both individuals and worldwide businesses will consume goods and services in ways that bring the most satisfaction.

"Economics is the study of how individuals and groups make decisions about what to produce and what to consume."

Based on how well a certain item sells, restaurants decide whether to offer more of it. Economics is the study of how individuals and groups make decisions about what to produce and what to consume. It also involves studying how these decisions affect one another.

Microeconomics is based on the economic decisions of individuals and businesses. Macroeconomics considers a broader range of elements, which can affect trade throughout the world. In macroeconomics, economists look at the whole economy, including governments and countries. When government officials try to help the economy grow, they look to principles of macroeconomics.

2 Supply and Demand

Within each industry, the forces of supply and demand determine prices and set trends for the amount of goods or services that will be produced or offered. The managers of a passenger airline company, for example, have to decide how much to charge for each seat on each flight.

The supply of airline tickets is based, to some degree, on the number of seats in each plane and the number of flights each plane can make. The supply of something, how much people want it, and how many people are able to pay for it all help to determine its price. The supply of airline seats can be compared with the demand for tickets or seats.

During holiday seasons, the demand for seats rises, as more people travel. This is one reason why many airlines raise their prices for flights during holiday periods. In general, higher prices can be set for goods or services that many people want or cannot do without. Quite often, the opposite is also true. Prices tend to be lower when there is a large supply of something compared to the amount people want or need. This is why airlines often have special sales at times of year when fewer people tend to travel.

When stores offer new products, such as electronics, demand among consumers can be high.

Economists take a scientific view of supply, demand, and related forces. World trade is made up of many businesses making decisions that have wide-reaching effects. To make predictions and recommendations, economists look at trading factors that are related together.

In the example of the airline company, managers do not just set the price of tickets. They also make decisions regarding **resources**, such as how much fuel to buy and how many workers to employ. They may buy fuel manufactured in different parts of the world. In addition, they may have employees working at international airports. An economist looking at airlines studies fuel and labor markets across the world.

Does Economics Matter to People Outside Business or Politics?

Discussions about economics often focus on businesses and governments, which consider group concerns when setting policies. Businesses and governments must achieve goals that involve large numbers of people. Stores, for example, need to decide how much to charge for each item being sold. Government officials may have to decide whether to impose a higher tax on goods that flow in from a neighboring country.

The economy, however, involves everyone. Individuals play a direct role by working or not working and by making purchases or deciding not to buy certain items. People can also affect the economy by voting for politicians who share their beliefs about how the economy should operate.

Teachers of Economics
We work to make sure people understand the economy. If they understand how it works, people can better make financial choices and vote for leaders and policies that benefit everyone.

Local Bankers
Economics can be complicated. Our business is to help people deal with some of the confusing aspects of money and the economy. We can help people figure out the best ways to make and save money.

Young Job Seekers
We are busy looking for work. We do not have time to think about the nation's economy, much less the world economy. Economic issues are important, but we simply cannot think about them now.

Frustrated Individuals
Businesses and the government seem to decide how the economy works. The issues are complicated and hard to understand. Besides, we cannot influence them.

For   Supportive   Undecided   Unsupportive   Against

3 Capital

In world trade, each nation has strengths and resources. Canada is rich in forests and minerals. Russia has large deposits of oil and coal. Nations with large supplies of such natural resources often sell some to other countries, use some themselves, and turn the rest into various products. These goods may be sold in the nation where they are made or to other countries.

Producing goods usually requires three types of resources. They are land, labor, and capital. When economists talk about land, they mean all the resources that are tied to Earth, including plants, animals, and the energy that comes from natural resources. Labor is the work people do to produce things and turn natural resources into products. Capital is the tools and structures needed for production.

There are many types of capital. Capital includes physical assets, such as baking ovens and factories. There is human capital, or the skills and knowledge that workers bring to their jobs. Capital can also be money. Businesses need owners or investors, who put their money into the enterprise. Investors may be anywhere in the world. Capital, as well as goods, can move from country to country.

A **stock market** provides companies with ways to get capital. In a stock market, people buy shares in businesses. A share of stock represents a share in company ownership, and people trade shares based on the changing values of the stock. A stock market is only one type of financial market. A financial market is any market where buyers and sellers trade some kind of financial asset, or something of value.

Timber, which is one of Canada's natural resources, is used to produce goods such as furniture and paper.

4 Free and Protected Trade

The gross domestic product, or GDP, of a nation is the value of its goods and services. In early 2013, the GDP of the United States was approximately $16 trillion. That represented about 25 percent of the total world economy.

GDP has four parts. The first part is the goods and services consumed by households. The second part is investments. The third part is the goods and services consumed by the government. The fourth part is the worth of **exports** minus **imports**.

Both businesses and governments look at the balance between imports and exports. Countries that export more than they import have trade surpluses. Countries that import more than they export have trade deficits.

Nations enter trade agreements with other nations that are often a mix **free trade** and **protectionism**. In free trade, stronger companies tend do better. Yet, some businesses benefit from protective measures, at least for a certain length of time.

World trade encourages the countries that can produce certain goods and services at the lowest cost to do so. This allows other nations to concentrate on producing other goods and services that they are the best at creating. Many economists believe that world trade allows living conditions to improve in most trading nations.

Technology can help countries raise GDP and compete. This is because with technology, countries can get more products out of resources. For example, silicon, which is found in sand, can be used to make the chips that run computers and many other electronic devices.

Countries that produce more oil than they need can export some to other nations.

5 Developed and Developing Countries

In world trade, there is a clear divide between developed nations, with high living standards, and developing nations, with little industry. To track world trade and its results, the United Nations (UN) divides the world into five major regions. They are Africa, the Americas, Asia, Europe, and Oceania.

The UN further describes nations as developed or developing. The developed nations include Japan, Canada, the United States, and most countries in Europe. Developing nations include many island states, African nations, and eastern European countries.

As of 2014, the UN called 48 nations "least developed." According to the UN, people in these nations have poor nutrition, health, and education. The economic systems in these countries are not strong or secure.

The UN identifies these nations using a measure called the Human Assets Index, which looks at the number of people who do not get enough food, the number of children who die before age 5, the number of people who are in school, and how many adults can read. The UN also has a measure called the Economic Vulnerability Index. This considers the size of the population and the stability of its exports and food production, among other factors.

When one part of the world is unstable, political problems and armed conflicts often occur. They may affect trade in that region. This can, in turn, affect the entire world. To maintain stability and prevent international problems, developed nations often invest in less developed lands.

United Nations Least Developed Nations, 2014

Africa			Asia	The Americas
Angola	Ethiopia	Rwanda	Afghanistan	Haiti
Benin	Gambia	São Tomé and Príncipe	Bangladesh	
Burkina Faso	Guinea	Senegal	Bhutan	
Burundi	Guinea-Bissau	Sierra Leone	Cambodia	
Central African Republic	Lesotho	Somalia	Kiribati	
Chad	Liberia	South Sudan	Laos	
Comoros	Madagascar	Sudan	Myanmar	
Democratic Republic of the Congo	Malawi	Tanzania	Nepal	
	Mali	Togo	Solomon Islands	
Djibouti	Mauritania	Uganda	Timor Leste	
Equatorial Guinea	Mozambique	Zambia	Tuvalu	
Eritrea	Niger		Vanuatu	
			Yemen	

Does the Developed World Have Responsibilities Toward the Developing World?

Developed nations benefit from having large companies that take resources from developing countries. This includes the use of cheaper labor. Some people think that companies that take resources from other lands should also give something back.

Recent events have complicated the issue, however. During the first decade of the 21st century, the world economy suffered a serious downturn, with high levels of unemployment. Even developed nations have struggled.

Development Groups

Many people in developing nations need clean water, food, and medicine. We all have a moral right to have our basic needs fulfilled, and it is our shared responsibility to aid those who need help.

Activists in Developing Countries

Our governments must take some responsibility for our economies, but international financial institutions are responsible, too. Banks charge our people higher fees than they charge in developed nations.

Economic Conservatives

Let charities or other special groups address specific needs in developing countries. In some instances, we may wish to help people in other countries, but it is not our responsibility. It is also not their right to demand our help.

Isolationists

No help should be given to other countries. In the past, when such aid was given, it was often wasted or even taken by dishonest leaders. It is not our responsibility to save the world. We need to make our own country stronger.

| For | Supportive | Undecided | Unsupportive | Against |

Development of Trade

Nations have been trading since ancient times, but world trade increased a great deal after World War II (1939–1945). When this war ended, many people hoped to create a community of nations that would work together for peace and economic development. Ever since, trade has grown quickly, sped by improvements in the transporting of goods and the ease of world travel. Not all nations, however, have enjoyed the benefits equally.

1 Bretton Woods and the IMF

As World War II was drawing to a close, representatives from 50 nations met in San Francisco, California, to form the United Nations. They signed the UN Charter in June 1945. Even before then, in July 1944, delegates from 44 **Allied nations** met at the Bretton Woods Conference in New Hampshire. They hoped to create favorable conditions for trade to help the world's recovery.

The Bretton Woods Agreement changed the world trade system in historic ways. The Allies agreed to recognize an international system of **currencies**, making it easier to conduct trade. They also decided to make money convertible. This means that money could be converted to something of value, such as gold.

In the interest of shared economic goals, the nations further agreed to fixed **exchange rates**. They also formed several organizations, such as the International Monetary Fund (IMF), the International Trade Organization (ITO), and the World Bank. All this helped to lay the basis for a system of free trade.

In 2014, the IMF had 188 member countries. Its mission is to promote global growth and economic stability. It supports international cooperation on financial matters and helps member nations that are having financial problems. The IMF also works with developing nations to help them achieve economic stability and reduce poverty.

The European economy was weak following World War II. A great deal of property, including factories, had been destroyed.

2 World Bank

The World Bank is not an ordinary bank. It is an international institution that creates policies regarding economics and trade. In early 2014, the World Bank had 188 member nations, including the United States. The World Bank provides help to the world's nations. Workers at the bank give information and advice about trends in the world economy.

In recent years, the organization's officials have identified two main goals. The first is to decrease the number of people living on less than $1.25 per day to no more than 3 percent of the world's population. The second is to help increase the incomes of the poorest 40 percent of population in each nation. Bank officials have set the year 2030 as their target for these goals.

The World Bank has two main parts. The first is the International Bank for Reconstruction and Development (IBRD), which lends money to nations with middle or low incomes. The second part is the International Development Association (IDA), which offers loans with no interest to poor countries.

The World Bank Group is separate from the World Bank. The World Bank Group refers to a number of organizations that work together to reduce poverty. The World Bank Group is made up of the IBRD, the IDA, and three other organizations that help with investments.

Global Poverty by Region, 2010

The World Bank identifies anyone living on $1.25 per day or less as being in poverty. The percentage of people who are that poor varies in different regions. The bank's statistics do not include nations of the developed world.

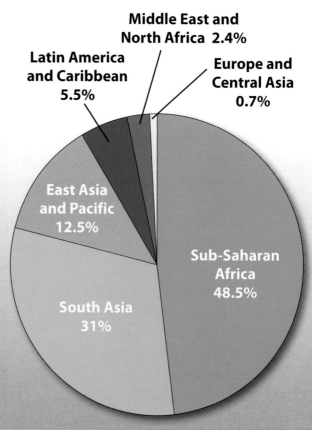

Middle East and North Africa 2.4%

Latin America and Caribbean 5.5%

Europe and Central Asia 0.7%

East Asia and Pacific 12.5%

Sub-Saharan Africa 48.5%

South Asia 31%

ECONOMIC ISSUE

Is Free Trade the Best Means of Trading?

A government with a free trade policy does little, or even nothing, to affect the number or kind of imports and exports. In a totally free trade situation, nations trade goods without **tariffs**. There are no taxes or other policies meant to control trade. Prices are set by supply and demand, and some companies win while others lose. One of the first people to promote free trade was the 18th century economist Adam Smith. He was a pioneer in economic thinking who believed that free trade would lead to better social and economic conditions.

Conservative Economists

Yes. History has shown that free trade provides opportunities for increased growth and profits. It also allows each nation to develop the products and jobs that country is best suited to create.

Industrialists

Increased trade means increased cooperation. In the end, this is one of the most important ways of keeping nations from going to war. Free trade also tends to help business, increase job opportunities, and reduce poverty.

Anti-Globalists

The greatest benefits of free trade go to the wealthy, such as big business owners and investors in the financial markets. Also, when economies are dependent on global markets, they are more vulnerable to downturns in the economies of their trading partners.

Advocates for U.S. Jobs

Jobs are being lost in the United States because other countries, such as China, can pay lower wages and produce goods for a far lower cost. To save U.S. jobs, we need policies designed to keep cheap goods out of the country and to create jobs here at home.

For   Supportive   Undecided   Unsupportive   Against

3 GATT

A number of economic agreements built the framework of modern trade. One of most important pacts occurred in 1947, when UN delegates developed the original General Agreement on Tariffs and Trade (GATT). To encourage trade, officials from 23 countries pledged to stop charging various tariffs.

The UN delegates hoped to lead by example and discourage protectionism. Protectionists often give tax breaks to their own businesses and charge tariffs on goods from other countries. Sometimes, they provide **subsidies** to favored businesses. They may also impose **import quotas**.

The GATT delegates were unhappy with protectionism because of events they had lived through. The United States and other countries had used protectionist measures in the 1930. Many economists believed these measures made economic conditions worse during the **Great Depression**. Widespread hardship during the Depression may have helped lead to World War II.

In the 1920s, there had been a boom in the value of stocks in many U.S. companies. Investors in the stock market grew wealthier, but more than half of Americans were poor. With few people to buy goods, many U.S. businesses found themselves with unsold items.

> "Many economists believed that protectionist measures made conditions worse during the Great Depression."

By the late 1920s, many people believed that stock prices were too high. They did not accurately reflect the worth of U.S. businesses. In October 1929, there was a sudden rush to sell shares of stock in U.S. companies. In this so-called stock market crash, the price of shares dropped sharply. Many investors lost large amounts of money.

A widespread feeling of panic about economic conditions followed. People tended to buy even fewer goods than before the crash, and many companies suffered losses or went out of business. People lost their jobs.

In an effort to help U.S. companies sell more goods, the government used tariffs to keep out foreign products. However, other countries also adopted tariffs. As a result, businesses around the world could not export goods. The economies of many countries suffered, and even more people were out of work.

4 Uruguay Round

One of the GATT's original purposes was to set up an international trade organization as a key part of the UN system. Members of the U.S. Congress rejected this part of the plan, however. For more than 40 years, the GATT functioned as a set of international trading rules. There was no related regulatory organization.

During those years, the GATT underwent various rounds of revisions. Each time, the member nations agreed to more tariff reductions. Eventually, they also agreed to reductions in subsidies for agriculture, as a way to manage the world food supply.

Over time, member nations came to realize that the GATT rules were not enough to deal with all world trade issues. It was time to create an actual authority for world trade. In 1986, representatives met in Uruguay. Under the terms of the Uruguay Round of negotiations, the members agreed to set up the World Trade Organization (WTO). To become a member of the WTO, a nation needed to accept the standards set out in the Uruguay Round.

In 1947, the GATT had included 23 nations. The Uruguay Round involved more than 100 countries. Most were developing countries, including some of the poorest. The WTO declared the Uruguay Round "the largest trade negotiation ever."

From 1950 to the present, world trade issues have continued to evolve. Reducing tariffs remains important. Agreements in other areas of business are now getting more focus, however. WTO nations discuss important issues related to agriculture, telecommunications, financial services, **information technology**, and **intellectual property**.

When the Uruguay Round was completed, delegates from the countries involved had to sign numerous documents on the agreements they had reached.

Trade Organization

... is not a world government that tells countries what policies to create. It is, instead, an organization based on consensus. The entire group reaches decisions about trade policies. The WTO's stated goal is to enable "open, fair, and undistorted competition." The member nations create rules meant to benefit them all.

In practice, however, many countries try to advance their own national interests. Occasionally, some nations take advantage of loopholes in the WTO rules. These are errors in the rules that make it possible to legally avoid obeying them.

When disagreements arise, the group holds negotiations, which can help make relationships between nations better. Being part of a group helps countries in conflict address their problems in a neutral way. **Bilateral** negotiations, by contrast, can easily lead to political confrontation. In this way, the WTO contributes to world peace as well as economic order.

Today, the majority of WTO members are developing countries or former **communist** countries. Many of them have loosened trade restrictions in recent years. More and more developing countries are building successful industrial economies.

Like the members of the GATT that preceded it, the WTO members are committed to helping developing countries. In practice, however, this goal is not always followed. A number of developing countries have prospered. Overall, however, the income gaps between wealthy and poor countries appear to be increasing.

World's Largest Exporters and Importers of Goods

In 2012, a few countries led the world as exporters and importers of goods.

Rank	Exporters	Value in billions of U.S. dollars	% of World Total	Rank	Importers	Value in billions of U.S. dollars	% of World Total
1	China	2,049	11.1	1	United States	2,336	12.6
2	United States	1,546	8.4	2	China	1,818	9.8
3	Germany	1,407	7.6	3	Germany	1,167	6.3
4	Japan	799	4.3	4	Japan	886	4.8
5	Netherlands	656	3.6	5	United Kingdom	690	3.7
6	France	569	3.1	6	France	674	3.6
7	South Korea	548	3.0	7	Netherlands	591	3.2

Should Nations Join Together to Form Trade Groups?

Members of the WTO work together to make decisions about how world trade operates. Other types of trade groups exist as well. Trade blocs are sets of countries, such as nations in the same region, that enter into agreements to take part in trade together. People disagree about whether large trade groups are always a good idea. Some feel that countries should act on their own when it comes to trade.

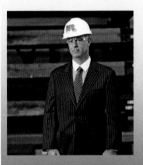

Advocates of Globalization

The power of the WTO is used for the shared good. The Generalized System of Preferences is a plan that grants the poorest countries special trade conditions. This system is a key part of the WTO.

Leaders of Trade Blocs

Joining together is a way to help poorer nations succeed. The rich, industrialized countries still dominate world trade, but they no longer make all of the rules alone.

Political Skeptics

Sometimes, joining together backfires. When trading blocs act in their own short-term self-interest, this can reduce the power of individual nations that might do better acting in a different way. At times, less powerful nations in a trading bloc must go along with plans that can hurt them.

U.S. Protectionists

We should avoid entering into long-term commitments to other countries and allowing other nations to dictate how we conduct trade. Joining an international trade group can make a nation that works against our nation's full competitiveness to us.

For   Supportive   Undecided   Unsupportive   Against

Trade in Action

KEY CONCEPTS

1 European Union

2 NAFTA

3 APEC

4 Cairns Group

5 Group of 20

The WTO involves countries in many parts of the world. Other trade groups focus on specific regions or types of trade. In many of these groups, members set trade rules. Pressure from other countries in the organization, rather than laws, makes members obey the rules.

1 European Union

The countries in a trading bloc promote trade among themselves. Tariffs and customs procedures, or the way goods enter and leave each country, are usually the same within the bloc. This makes it easier for members to trade with one another. Trading blocs promote economic activity and closer relations among member states. Another purpose of a trading bloc is to strengthen its powers of negotiation with external parties.

The European Union (EU) is a single market of 28 European nations. In general, goods, services, money, and people can move from one EU country to another without restrictions. This stimulates trade. More than half of the imports and exports of EU countries come from or go to other member states.

To further promote trade, the EU created its own currency, called the euro. It is used by about two-thirds of EU countries. When nations share the same currency, a business in one country does not have to exchange money for another currency in order to pay for imported goods.

The EU has broad social aims, as well as economic goals. Some poorer EU countries, such as Spain, Portugal, Ireland, and Greece, have obtained **grants** from the EU to help them develop their economies. However, the organization also can require members to follow certain economic policies. Members such as Greece and Spain have been forced to sharply reduce government spending because they had borrowed large amounts of money. The spending cuts have led to unemployment and other hardships in these countries.

The euro, introduced in 1999, is currently used by more than 333 million people in the EU.

Mapping World Trade

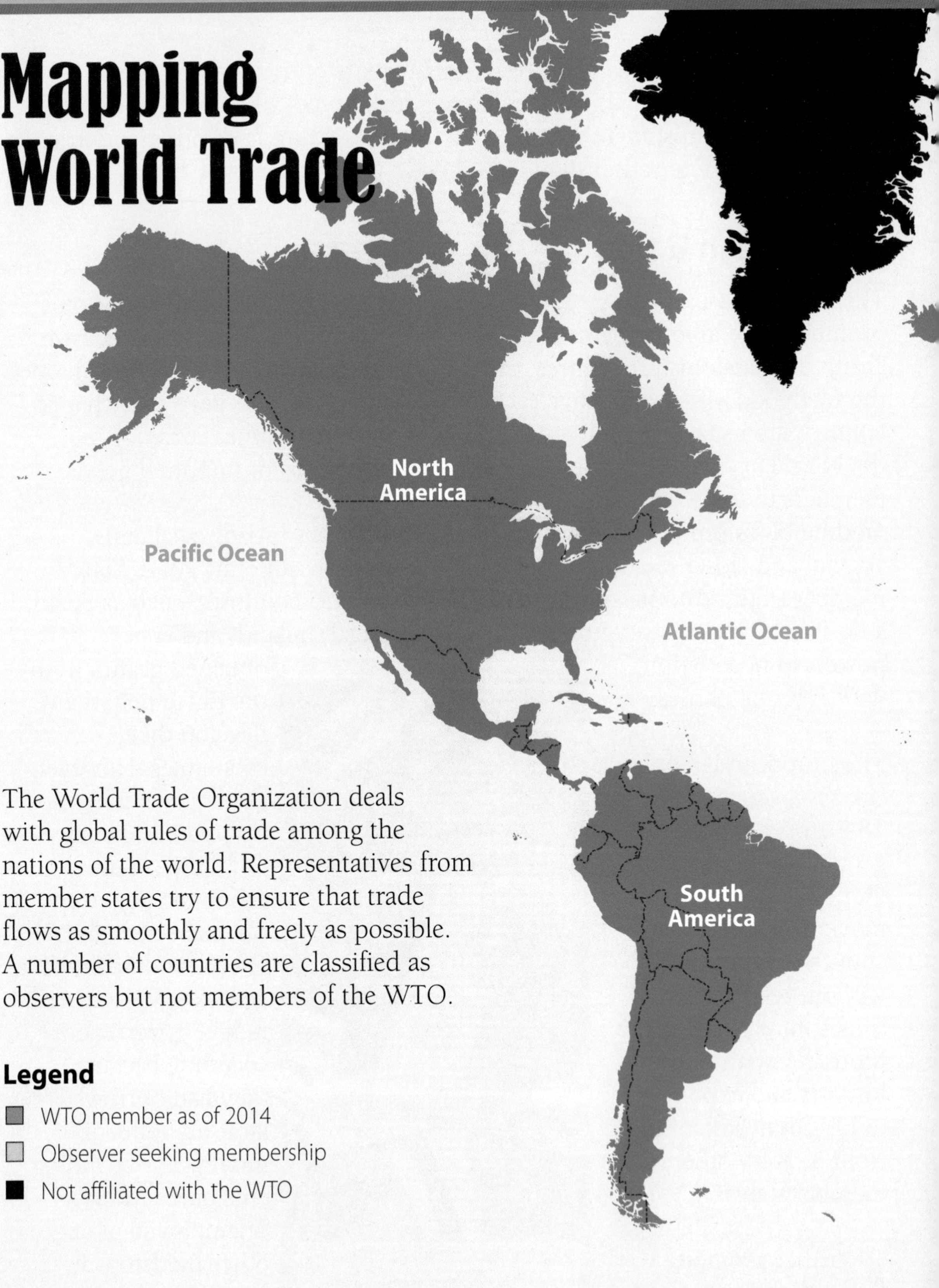

North America

Pacific Ocean

Atlantic Ocean

The World Trade Organization deals with global rules of trade among the nations of the world. Representatives from member states try to ensure that trade flows as smoothly and freely as possible. A number of countries are classified as observers but not members of the WTO.

South America

Legend

- WTO member as of 2014
- Observer seeking membership
- Not affiliated with the WTO

2 NAFTA

NAFTA stands for the North American Free Trade Agreement. It is an agreement between the United States, Mexico, and Canada. Since NAFTA went into effect in 1994, the three nations have gradually reduced their tariffs and other limits on imports from one another. The agreement has both supporters and critics.

Supporters say that eliminating trade barriers among the North American countries benefits this part of the world. For example, food is now bought and sold more freely between Canada, the United States, and Mexico. In addition, some areas of Mexico have seen an increase in manufacturing since NAFTA was enacted.

In the United States, however, some critics of NAFTA are concerned about food imports. They argue that laws to protect the environment and health are not always well enforced in Mexico. As a result, it is possible that imported food items may have chemicals on them that are not allowed in the United States.

Workers in Mexico, on average, earn lower wages than workers in the United States. This means that products made in Mexico and exported to the United States may be inexpensive for Americans to buy.

Consumers in the United States may save money.

However, lower wages in Mexico may cause some U.S. manufacturing companies to close factories in the United States and open new ones in Mexico instead. These companies can save money on wages and then easily bring the goods produced into the United States to be sold. The companies' former U.S. workers, though, have lost their jobs. In addition, companies that keep factories in the United States may use the possibility of moving jobs to Mexico as a way to keep their U.S. workers from asking for wage increases.

Mexican farmers protested against NAFTA because it led to corn from the United States being sold cheaply in Mexico. This reduced the price of corn there and forced some Mexican farmers out of business.

Do the Needs of a Nation's Regional Trade Partners Override Other International Interests?

Many people support trade tactics that promote their own country. It can also make sense for a country to give support to nations in the same region. Aiding neighboring countries helps keep a region stable. Countries enter into regional trade agreements to improve their security and gain access to larger markets for their goods.

Regional Trade Advocates

Regional trade agreements can be very beneficial and solve many problems. NAFTA, for example, has made it easier for the partner countries to link their energy supplies. The more business one partner does, the better for all.

Anti-Globalists

The buildup of global powers like international trade groups can hurt local and sometimes regional interests. National, ethnic, and religious identities are maintained better through regional groups.

Advocates of Transatlantic Trade

Recent economic issues are forcing countries to rethink their trade agreements and look at broader interests. One possible outcome may be that the EU and the United States enter a special agreement that would benefit Europe and the United States.

Supporters of Global Trade

Nations involved in regional trade agreements may take a view that is too narrow. By concentrating on their regional partners, these nations may ignore the economic benefits of trading with the rest of the world. A more global view of trade is better for the entire world.

For   Supportive   Undecided   Unsupportive   Against

3 APEC

The United States conducts trade under various agreements, joining with other nations for different reasons. NAFTA is one agreement affecting U.S. trade. The United States also takes part in the Asia-Pacific Economic Cooperation (APEC) group.

APEC identifies itself as a forum, which is a place or opportunity for discussion of a topic. According to APEC, its primary goal is to support sustainable economic growth and prosperity in the Asia-Pacific region. Its 21 members include Australia, China, Japan, the United States, Russia, and Canada. Most agreed to join together in 1989. They have since worked to eliminate trade barriers and to establish the Pacific as a trading region.

The group created a Trade Facilitation Action Plan among member nations, which reduced the cost of trade in the region by 5 percent from 2002 to 2006. A second Trade Facilitation Action Plan cut the costs of regional trade by another 5 percent between 2007 and 2010. The group works on other issues besides trade. Representatives also discuss matters such as actions the group can take to protect members against terrorism.

Some critics of APEC argue that the group has been too concerned with political issues. They say APEC should focus more on promoting trade and establishing the region as an even greater force in the global economy. Others critics say that bilateral agreements that some of APEC's members make go against any work the group has done together.

Despite criticism, the forum continues to advance its free trade goals. In 2014, the group was working on the Trans-Pacific Partnership Agreement, to manage trade in the region. Meanwhile, the Association of Southeast Asian Nations (ASEAN) works toward similar agreements. Its 10 members are all located in Southeast Asia.

APEC projects have turned waste from sugarcane stalks into energy sources in Thailand.

4 Cairns Group

The Cairns Group is an organization of 19 countries that export crops. Unlike regional groups, Cairns has members in Latin America, Africa, and the Asia-Pacific area. They represent both developed and developing nations, and they work together to increase trade in agricultural products.

The group formed in 1986, when members met in Cairns, Australia. They worked together at the Uruguay Round negotiations later that year. Until then, developed countries charged high tariffs on food coming in from elsewhere and paid subsidies to their own farmers. As a result, these countries often had food surpluses that they shipped to other nations. This made it difficult for farmers in less-developed lands to profit from growing and selling their own crops.

Since then, the WTO has been mindful of the effects of crop subsidies. Agriculture is now viewed as an important part of world trade agreements. Opening markets and lowering tariffs have yielded billions of dollars more per year in income from agricultural exports.

Coffee growers in Colombia are among the people who have been helped by the work of the Cairns Group.

Barriers remain in place, however, especially when it comes to trade in agriculture. After the Uruguay Round, some nations "cheated" by raising tariffs before reducing them. This was similar to the way a store raises prices by 10 percent before holding a sale in which prices are cut by 10 percent. Because of subsidies that were put in place, the domestic consumers of Japanese rice and Swiss butter, for example, have paid several times more than the world market prices of rice and butter. Restrictions on farm-product imports have often been phased out over a much longer period than limits on industrial goods.

5 Group of 20

The Group of 20, or G-20, is a group of nations that joined together after a crisis in international finance in the late 1990s. The problem began when there were problems with Southeast Asian financial markets. The crisis then spread to other markets, including the U.S. market.

Soon after the U.S. stock market crashed, banks in Japan and Korea did not have enough money on hand to function, so they failed. In mid-1998, Russia's financial market crashed as well. Similar problems spread to Latin America.

These developments showed that problems in one part of the world could dramatically affect markets on the other side of the planet. They also demonstrated that global finance was vulnerable. To try to avoid similar crises, representatives from seven industrial countries joined together in the fall of 1999. The group continues to meet to discuss reforms for international finance and to strengthen the financial system.

The G-20 now includes 19 nations and the EU. The United States, Canada, and Russia are among the members. The G-20 nations represent approximately 85 percent of global GDP and more than 75 percent of global trade. They also represent some two-thirds of the population of the world.

Helping developing countries is one of the G-20's goals. This would improve conditions in those countries. It would also make it possible for them to contribute to trade and economic growth in the rest of the world.

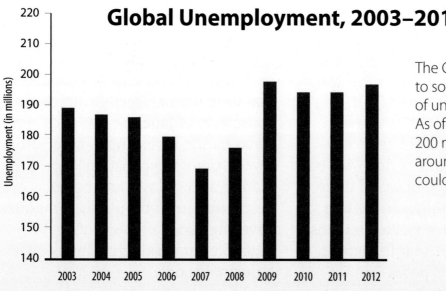

Global Unemployment, 2003–2012

The G-20 is working to solve problems of unemployment. As of 2012, almost 200 million workers around the world could not find jobs.

Should Trade Groups Be Allowed to Regulate Corporations?

Many people believe that business decisions that promote free trade lead to greater wealth and prosperity. However, continuing poverty in the developing world and unemployment in developed nations have raised doubts about trade decisions made by corporations. Corporations are judged by how much profit they make. Yet, decisions that increase profits may not benefit workers and consumers. Some people say that international trade groups should regulate corporations, which do not always make wise decisions.

Trade Groups
Regulations that are part of global agreements have not been harmful to corporations. Manufacturers have been able to work with developing countries, where they can pay lower wages. This has helped the corporations to profit, while also providing jobs in those countries.

Liberal Politicians
The hope is that the WTO and groups like it can create agreements that help to spread good employment and production practices around the world. The trading coalitions are here to protect people from companies when this is necessary.

U.S. Business Groups
Businesses operate best when looking out for their own interests. We are the only people who understand exactly what issues we face.

Conservative Politicians
Our corporations do not need advice or rules from international groups. We can best help our people ourselves, because we know our own problems. Let our businesspeople do what they can to employ people and make money.

| For | Supportive | Undecided | Unsupportive | Against |

Issues of Trade

KEY CONCEPTS

1 Labor Standards

2 Environmental Issues

3 International Cooperation

Global trade increases both business opportunities and competitive pressures. In some cases, increased trade has led to lower wages and worse working conditions. To address these problems, some people are calling for a minimum code of labor standards in all trade agreements. Other people want regulation of industries known to harm the environment.

1 Labor Standards

The *maquiladoras* of Mexico are factories that are owned by foreigners, often U.S. companies. Employees may work six days per week in 10-hour shifts with few breaks. Working conditions may be unsafe. The factories have been getting special lower taxes from the Mexican government.

Some people warn that global trade encourages these kinds of conditions. Others say a global economy brings new awareness of labor issues and the need for standards. The International Labour Organization (ILO) and other groups work to educate people about their rights and labor standards. The ILO wants the minimum working age in most circumstances to be 15.

The United Nations Children's Fund (UNICEF) has a goal of ending the worst forms of child labor abuses by 2016. In 2011, UNICEF estimated that there were 215 million children under age 18 working around the world. In Sub-Saharan Africa, one in four children aged 5 to 17 were working.

2 Environmental Issues

Many developed countries have adopted "green" standards to protect the environment in their own area, such as measures to keep air and water clean. Sometimes, however, developed countries have actually sent their waste elsewhere. Hazardous waste is sometimes "exported" from developed countries, only to be dumped in developing lands.

In this way, rich countries are harming poor countries. The developing countries cannot afford to adopt the kinds of anti-pollution measures found in developed countries. Regulating these green issues is not easy. One country is not allowed to impose its own laws on another nation.

As of 2014, the WTO had no specific agreement in place dealing with the environment. Still, protecting and preserving the environment is one of the WTO's goals. Recent negotiations have specifically discussed environmental issues, with the aim of supporting both trade and the environment.

3 International Cooperation

International trade organizations do not always help the environment. In 1991, for example, a GATT panel prohibited the United States from forcing its own rules for dolphin-friendly fishing on Mexico. The Mexican boats, fishing for tuna, were using nets that often captured and killed dolphins. In the end, Mexico and the United States held bilateral meetings to work through the issue.

More recently, the United States banned imports of shrimp caught in ways that did not protect **endangered** turtles. A WTO panel upheld the ban in 2001. This was, in part, because the United States had tried to negotiate a treaty to protect turtles.

In general, however, the WTO argues that social and environmental matters are best left out of trade negotiations. Instead, the WTO says that these issues should be addressed in separate international agreements. Despite this WTO position, trade policies have become involved in disputes about environmental and social issues.

Sometimes, measures that protect the environment can hurt trade, yet world leaders agree that it is still necessary for them to take action in such cases. For example, steps have been taken to limit the transportation of dangerous materials across national borders. Many nations have also agreed to do what they can to stop the trade in endangered species.

Factory workers in China often have poor working conditions and earn low pay.

Should Children Around the World Be Protected by the Same Labor Standards?

Some people believe that labor standards need to be included in world trade agreements. Labor standards are regulations intended to protect workers. These regulations may prevent child labor. Standards can also provide for a safe, healthful workplace and decent wages.

Children's Aid Groups

All children should be getting an education, not working to earn money. We must protect children in the United States and around the world. Many farmworkers are children, using dangerous pesticides and machines.

World Trade Lobbyists

Children are working in dangerous conditions in factories, fields, and mines. The ILO has relatively little power to deal with this. The WTO should work to enforce labor standards, especially related to children.

International Aid Workers

A worldwide ban on child labor might sound like a good idea, but it could make matters worse. It could drive struggling families further into poverty. The overall idea is right, but such a ban must be put in place slowly and carefully.

Social Workers

Education is needed about this issue, on both sides. Many labor violations have little to do with international trade. In many countries, child labor is a normal part of family life. Some children work safely with their relatives in family businesses, such as small shops.

For   Supportive   Undecided   Unsupportive   Against

World Trade through History

Throughout history, people have bartered, trading one thing for another as needed. Eventually, humans invented mediums of exchange. They began trading items that represented value, such as salt, tea, or seashells. About 5,000 years ago, money became the medium of trade, first as coins and precious metals and eventually as paper currency.

138 BC
A Chinese expedition led by Zhang Qian opens a trade route to the West.

1500 AD
European trade empires begin to form.

1944
The Bretton Woods Conference sets up the International Trade Organization, the International Monetary Fund, and an international bank.

1948
The General Agreement on Tariffs and Trade goes into effect, enforcing rules through dispute settlement. Various rounds of GATT trade negotiations follow.

1957
West Germany, France, Italy, the Netherlands, Belgium, and Luxembourg sign the Treaty of Rome, establishing a trading bloc, called the European Economic Community.

1944

1994

1986
The Uruguay Round of GATT trade talks begins.

1994
The North American Free Trade Agreement goes into effect. The agreement includes Canada, Mexico, and the United States.

1995
The World Trade Organization, established by GATT in 1994, begins functioning.

1997

WTO members agree to eliminate customs duties and other charges on information technology products by the year 2000. Duties and charges are also eliminated on trade in banking, insurance, securities, and financial information. An other agreement expands trade in basic telecommunications.

1999

The third WTO Ministerial Conference is held in Seattle, Washington. Protesters claim the WTO fails to help poor people or protect the environment.

2002

2001

The WTO launches the Doha Round of trade talks in Qatar. The nations meet at near-annual intervals through 2008.

2002

A dozen European countries establish the euro as the currency they all will use.

2008

The Doha Round of trade talks collapses when the United States, China, and India cannot agree on the means of protecting poor farmers.

2013

Doha trade talks continue. In December, nations agree on the Bali Package, the first comprehensive agreement in the WTO's history.

1999

Working in World Trade

ECONOMIST

Duties Studies how society distributes resources, such as land, labor, and raw materials, to produce goods and services

Education A graduate degree for most jobs in the private sector

Interest The economy and how determining factors change it

Economists may work for insurance companies, banks, securities firms, industry and trade associations, labor unions, and other agencies. An economist who works for the government may study public policy or legislation. He or she may also look at the value of currency and its effect on imports and exports. Other typical duties include conducting surveys, interpreting data, preparing reports, and briefing news media, industry, and labor about economic trends. Economists may specialize in field such as advanced theory or labor economics. They generally work alone, but they are also part of research teams. Some travel for work.

LOBBYIST

Duties Convinces government officials to take a certain stand on specific issues

Education No specific education is required, but legal training is helpful

Interest Politics, an interest in particular groups or organizations

Lobbyists have varying experience, such as training in law, teaching, public relations, or journalism. A successful lobbyist must understand how the political system works. One place to learn about the legislative process is in a congressional office, where trainees can develop ties with the people making important decisions. The lobbyist must also be an expert on his or her chosen cause or organization. It is essential to understand the client's interests and the laws and policies the lobbyist hopes to influence. To succeed, a lobbyist must communicate effectively in both writing and speaking. He or she can work at the state or federal level.

LOGISTICIAN

Duties Analyzes and manages the supply chain for an organization

Education A bachelor's degree to reach beyond entry-level positions, and often a master's degree

Interest Business, making and executing plans to increase efficiency

Logisticians use software and other tools of management to move products from manufacturers and other suppliers to consumers. The work can be complex, so logisticians often have a master's degree in business, industrial engineering, or supply chain management. A logistician often directs the manner in which materials and finished products are dispersed, and figures out strategies to move goods with minimal cost and maximum efficiency. Many logisticians work for the federal government and the military, but they also work for shipping and manufacturing companies.

TRANSPORTATION COMPLIANCE OFFICER

Duties Evaluates whether individuals or organizations are conforming to laws and regulations related to transporting goods

Education An associate's or bachelor's degree in a related field and certification or special training

Interest Mechanical engineering, business management

Transportation inspectors use their mechanical skills and knowledge to ensure that the equipment used to transport goods, and sometimes the goods themselves, are in safe, working condition. Federal, state, and local governments employ inspectors in automotive, rail, air, or water transport. Aviation inspectors undergo special training from a school approved by the Federal Aviation Administration. An inspector's services are often required in architectural and engineering firms as well. Inspectors are called to the scene during accidents.

Key Trade Organizations

WTO

Goal Encourage fairness of trade competition, especially for poorer nations

Reach Worldwide

Facts It can take five years for a country to become a full member of the WTO

The World Trade Organization (WTO) expects members to open their markets to every other party on equal terms. This guiding principle reflects the belief that all WTO member nations have equal status and should not discriminate against one another. When trading partners agree on a tariff cut, the cut is automatically extended to all other WTO members. The group also promotes the idea of "national treatment," meaning that a foreign-owned company operating in a member state should be treated in the same way as a domestic company. The WTO holds rounds of negotiations, at which its members create trade agreements. WTO headquarters are in Geneva, Switzerland.

ILO

Goal Give equal voice to workers, employers, and governments

Reach Worldwide

Facts ILO headquarters are in Geneva, Switzerland, but there are field offices around the world

The International Labour Organization (ILO) has as its main goal the promotion of people's rights at work. To this end, the group promotes "decent employment opportunities" by holding talks among trade unions, employers, and government officials. Each member state sends delegates to represent its government, employers, and workers. Various heads of state address the ILO from time to time, and interested organizations attend the conferences as observers. The ILO was formed in 1919, after World War I. It became part of the United Nations in 1946.

USTR

Goal Develop and coordinate trade for the United States, overseeing negotiations

Reach Worldwide

Facts The USTR is part of the Executive Office of the President of the United States

The Office of the United States Trade Representative (USTR) coordinates trade policies for the United States and tries to expand U.S. trading opportunities. The office regularly publishes facts and data on ongoing issues, such as tobacco regulation, the cutting of tariffs, and new partnerships. The head of the USTR is a Cabinet member who advises the president and acts as the main spokesperson for related issues. Through the Trade Policy Review Group and the Trade Policy Staff Committee, the USTR also consults with other officials of government. The USTR works with Congress, often briefing committees.

WCO

Goal Protect security of and build capacity in customs agencies around the world

Reach Worldwide

Facts There are 179 members in the WCO, representing 98 percent of world trade

The World Customs Organization (WCO) is an international customs organization whose mission is to enhance the effectiveness and efficiency of customs administrations worldwide. A nation's customs is its agencies and procedures for inspecting, approving, and taxing imports and exports. The WCO assists and trains customs officials around the world. The group works to modernize customs offices. In its role as a monitor of trade, the group is often called on to combat fraud, piracy, and terrorism. The group was formed in 1952. Today, a council governs the WCO.

Research a World Trade Issue

The Issue

World trade is a subject of much debate. Groups may not always agree on the best ways to conduct world trade. It is important to enter a discussion to hear all the points of view before making decisions. Discussing issues will ensure that the actions taken are beneficial for all involved.

Get the Facts

Choose an issue (Political, Cultural, or Economic) from this book. Then, pick one of the four groups presented in the issue spectrum. Using the book and research in the library or on the Internet, find out more about the group you chose. What is important to members of this group? Why are they backing or opposing the particular issue? What claims or facts can they use to support their point of view? Be sure to write clear and concise supporting arguments for your group. Focus on world trade and the ways the group's needs relate to it. Will this group be affected in a positive or negative way by action taken related to world trade?

Use the Concept Web

A concept web is a useful research tool. Read the information and review the structure in the concept web on the next page. Use the relationships between concepts to help you understand your group's point of view.

Organize Your Research

Sort your information into organized points. Make sure your research answers clearly the impact the issue will have on your chosen group, how that impact will affect the group, and why the group has chosen the specific point of view.

WORLD TRADE CONCEPT WEB

Use this concept web to understand the network of factors contributing to issues related to world trade.

- Goods and services are exchanged worldwide
- Can benefits countries' economies
- Can build relationships between people, countries, and regions
- Trade developments have wide-ranging effects

- Job security
- Poverty levels
- Environment
- Forced labor
- Child labor
- Workers' rights

- Increases the amount of trade
- Can increase some people's incomes
- Countries specialize in goods and services they are best at producing

Social Issues

Benefits of Free Trade

Importance of Trade

WORLD TRADE

Drawbacks of Free Trade

World Trade Organization

Regional Trade Agreements

- May increase the gap between rich and poor
- Threat to some people's jobs and incomes
- High-wage economies must compete with low-wage economies

- Decisions are based on agreement among the member nations
- Goal is open and fair competition
- Solves problems through negotiations
- Committed to helping developing nations

- NAFTA   • EU
- APEC   • ASEAN

Test Your Knowledge

Answer each of the questions below to test your knowledge of the world trade issue.

1 What is the study of how people behave when making economic decisions?

2 What are the three main types of resources needed in production?

3 What does a share of stock represent?

4 What is the basic minimum working age that the ILO would like to see?

5 What is the term used for countries with low average income and little industry?

6 Name one of the first economists to promote free trade.

7 What organization did the GATT become?

8 What is the main trading bloc in Europe today?

9 What financial event caused the G-20 to form?

10 What is the trade agreement between the United States, Mexico, and Canada that went into effect in 1994?

ANSWERS 1. Microeconomics **2.** Land, labor, and capital **3.** A share in company ownership **4.** Age 15 **5.** Developing countries **6.** Adam Smith **7.** The World Trade Organization **8.** The European Union **9.** The financial crisis in 1997 and 1998 **10.** The North American Free Trade Agreement

Key Words

Allied nations: the nations that opposed Germany, Italy, Japan, and countries that fought on their side in World War II

bilateral: having to do with two countries or groups

communist: pertaining to societies in which the government owns the principal means of production and property is not owned privately

currencies: types of money, especially paper money

endangered: at risk of becoming extinct

exchange rates: numbers used to figure out the difference in value between the money used by various countries

exports: products sold to another country

free trade: trade in which governments do not interfere with or regulate imports and exports

grants: money given by a government, company, or group to be used for a particular purpose

Great Depression: the worldwide economic crisis beginning with the U.S. stock market crash in 1929 and continuing through the 1930s

import quotas: limits on the quantity of imports

imports: products brought into a country to be sold there

information technology: all forms of technology used to create, store, exchange, and use information

intellectual property: the results of a person's thoughts and creativity, including words, pictures, or music

protectionism: a government's placing of tariffs, quotas, or other restrictions on imports to protect domestic industries from global competition

resources: things a country uses to increase its wealth, such as land, labor, and capital

stock market: a place where stocks and similar items are bought and sold

subsidies: financial aid given by a government to individuals, companies, or groups

tariffs: taxes on imported goods and services

Index

Log on to www.av2books.com

AV² by Weigl brings you media enhanced books that support active learning. Go to www.av2books.com, and enter the special code found on page 2 of this book. You will gain access to enriched and enhanced content that supplements and complements this book. Content includes video, audio, weblinks, quizzes, a slide show, and activities.

AV² Online Navigation

Audio
Listen to sections of the book read aloud.

Book Pages
AV² pages directly correspond to pages in the book.

Video
Watch informative video clips.

Key Words
Study vocabulary, and complete a matching word activity.

Embedded Weblinks
Gain additional information for research.

Try This!
Complete activities and hands-on experiments.

Quizzes
Test your knowledge.

Slide Show
View images and captions, and prepare a presentation.

AV² was built to bridge the gap between print and digital. We encourage you to tell us what you like and what you want to see in the future.

Sign up to be an AV² Ambassador at www.av2books.com/ambassador.

Due to the dynamic nature of the Internet, some of the URLs and activities provided as part of AV² by Weigl may have changed or ceased to exist. AV² by Weigl accepts no responsibility for any such changes. All media enhanced books are regularly monitored to update addresses and sites in a timely manner. Contact AV² by Weigl at 1-866-649-3445 or av2books@weigl.com with any questions, comments, or feedback.